A User-Friendly Parish

"If I were responsible for convening a parish council I would gift each member with a copy of *A User Friendly Parish*. Then I would suggest that, as a pastoral community, we reflect on the book together, chapter by chapter, beginning with the last chapter and then moving on to the first. We would then have the benefit of a common framework for evaluating some aspects of our effectiveness. And who knows? We might be encouraged to change a few.

"This is a valuable resource for all kinds of parishes, large or small, rural or urban. Its message is for those who believe deeply in the value of their coming together for the sake of Christ's mission to the world."

—Dolores R. Leckey, Senior Fellow,
Woodstock Theological Center, Georgetown University.

"How do others see us? Any parish that really wants to know the answer to this question (and then honestly address what is learned) has to use this book. A comprehensive study and implementation of the principles and suggestions in this book will enhance every parish's efforts in evangelization, developing the sense of community, and deepening of commitment to the life and mission of the parish. A must read for all parish leaders."

—James J. DeBoy
Director of Leadership Development, Archdiocese of Baltimore

"Kollar is straightforward in rendering practical advice to parish leaders, staffs, and parishioners alike, inviting and encouraging everyone to examine how the parish presents itself. This little book promotes a simple, user-friendly method for becoming a more welcoming parish."

—Rev. Francis S. Tebbe, OFM
President of the National Organization for Continuing
Education of Roman Catholic Clergy
President of the Catholic Coalition on Preaching

"This is a workbook in the best sense of the word; a highly useful tool for parish staffs, volunteers, and leadership groups. Because it is so clearly and obviously practical, it is also eminently pastoral and loving."

—John Heagle, Co-Director
Therapy And Renewal Associates, Seattle, WA

"From simple acts of friendliness to ways of engaging parishioners with the wider world, this book is packed with pragmatic how-to lessons written in a style that both challenges and inspires."

—Elizabeth Brown
Diocesan Director of Communications, Diocese of Rochester

"With this book, parish councils/pastoral councils have a quick and easy 'user-friendly' self-evaluation at their fingertips to assist them in deepening the faith experience of their communities."

—Rev. Geoffrey Burke
Chancellor for Personnel, Diocese of Albany, NY

"This is a clear, concise, and 'on the mark' book about very real challenges. Kollar takes a no-nonsense approach to running committees with a purpose, meetings with an agenda, and finance councils with a clear understanding of the mission of the church. I look forward to the published book and recommending it to parish leaders."

—Kathleen Heffern
Director, Office of Church Ministry, Diocese of Buffalo

"Judith Kollar tells her readers exactly what hinders and helps the parish in becoming a 'welcoming community.' She does not mince words. She is simple, clear, and articulate."

—Sr. Angela Zukowski, MHSH, D.Min.
Director, Institute for Pastoral Initiatives
Unda World President

A User-Friendly
PARISH

Becoming a *More*
Welcoming Community

JUDITH ANN KOLLAR

FOREWORD BY FR. JOSEPH CHAMPLIN

TWENTY-THIRD PUBLICATIONS
Mystic, CT 06355

Second printing 1998

Twenty-Third Publications
185 Willow Street
P.O. Box 180
Mystic, CT 06355
(860) 536-2611
(800) 321-0411

ISBN 0-89622-937-8
Library of Congress Catalog Card Number 98-60700
Printed in the U.S.A.

DEDICATION

Nathan, Rudy
David and Sharon
Sunshine on my shoulders.

Foreword

In the August 1996 issue of the *Atlantic Monthly*, Charles Trueheart described a year-long study tour he made of giant, "full-service" megachurches throughout the United States. His lengthy essay, "Welcome to the Next Church," covers faith communities from Willow Grove and the Church of the Open Door in the mid-West, to Mariner's Church at Newport Beach, California, and the Fellowship of Las Colinas in Irving, Texas.

Similar ingredients or phenomena greeted him at each of these massive churches: ample parking, clear signage, clean bathrooms, attractive landscaping, cordial greeters. A warm, but respectful and non-intrusive welcoming attitude. Singable music. Relatable sermons. Inclusive worship. Countless and diverse services responding to their members' needs.

They all were user-friendly parishes.

The recently appointed rector of an East Coast cathedral experienced a parallel occurrence. During his initial months as shepherd of that church, he heard repeated complaints from local clergy about the music at diocesan functions. In his first year as rector, the priest made only minimal adjustments to their music program. He did, however, raise the maintenance budget and add a modest array of bushes and flowers around the front entrance. The cathedral looked more attractive on the outside and cleaner on the inside.

His clergy critics, curiously enough, now no longer complain about the music. Those basic user-friendly steps somehow dissolved their objections.

That cathedral rector and those megachurch pastors will applaud Judith Ann Kollar's first book, *A User-Friendly Parish: Becoming a More Welcoming Community*. It affirms what they are doing and offers them additional creative ways for further developing their already user-friendly parishes.

But pastoral leaders in all types of faith communities, huge or tiny, should also welcome this publication. It is an easy and fast read. It contains countless practical suggestions for making any parish a more welcoming community. It uses self-examination as a teaching tool. It has excellent discussion questions for each of the nine chapters.

I would envision clergy, pastoral staff personnel, and parish council members first reading *A User-Friendly Parish* as individuals. Then, as part of a particular group or committee, they could use the book on a monthly basis, chapter by chapter, for study and subsequent discussion stimulated by the questions provided.

These self-examination sessions will challenge participants and provoke thoughtful consideration, although the questions might make some people uneasy. Eventually, however, through honest reflection, response, and a decision to act readers will be empowered to make their particular faith community a more user-friendly and welcoming parish.

—*Rev. Joseph M. Champlin*

CONTENTS

A User-Friendly Parish

Introduction

In parishes all over the country (and, I suspect, the world), parish staff members, pastors, lay ministers, and concerned parishioners are asking themselves some variation of this question: how can we make our parish "better"? What can we do to engage more people in the life of the parish? How can our liturgies become more welcoming? Why are our programs not as successful as we want them to be? What—if anything—can we do about all this?

I believe that the answer to these questions involves some careful attending to the elements that would make the parish more user-friendly. These elements have little to do with what we believe about God, and more to do with how the parish exists as an entity in the world. Some of the elements involve simple common sense (which seems to be less and less common these days). Often, nothing more is required than simple thought and attention to detail.

In this book, I want to look at how the parish presents itself. I want to examine how people are invited to participate in programs, as well as how relevant the programs are to the real life of people. Other issues will be considered. How will someone be trained if they say "yes" to your request for volunteers? What does someone have to do to really be a member of the parish? How does the parish use its financial resources and how are these resources asked for? How inclusive is the community? Who is welcome here and how do people know they are welcome?

I will share with you experiences from parishes which might help you reflect on your own parish, and how to make it a more welcoming, user-friendly community. I will share questions that you can ask yourself to discover how your parish looks to a stranger and what you might do to make it more inviting. I will share stories of other congregations which may assist and inspire you in making some changes in your parish.

Try to get out and see other parishes; it's a great way to see what is going on in the Catholic church around the country. People who travel around, even if only to a few other local churches, have a broader perspective on what can be done and how it can be done. They also get a sense of whether they want to hurry back to their local parish or wish they could stay with this newly discovered community...and why.

I would be foolish if I said that what we believe about God and our faith doesn't count in what the parish becomes. Of course, things like whether the community is socially concerned, has meaningful homilies, and a modern liturgy make a difference. But there are fundamental elements that underlie the "coming together" and the "staying together" of a parish, and these elements will be the focus of this book.

Get ready, here come the questions.

CHAPTER ONE

Appearances Are Important

Let's pretend for a minute that you are in your car, looking for the local Catholic church. (You can make it your
own parish, if you would like.) How do you find the parish?
Are there signs in key places along the road directing you to
its location? If you stopped and asked for directions, would
the "locals" know where to send you?

Now you've found the church. You drive up to the building. Is there a sign on the lawn to identify this as St. Joachim
Parish? What else do you see? Does the building look
"friendly"? Cared for? Does it look like it will stand for a
while? Is the lawn cut? If it is spring or summer, are there
plantings and flowers visible?

Park the car and take a look. (How easy was it to find a place to park, by the way?) Is there any sign of life around the buildings? Get out of your car and walk to the door of the church. Is it open? If not, is there a sign telling people when the church will be open?

If the door is open, walk inside. Does the entrance look clean? Is the church in good order? Is there a rack of literature in the back of the church? What can you tell about the parish from the entryway? What signs of life are visible? Are there any pictures of real people? Is there a card or flyer available to tell people about the parish, its services, its history, and its current activities? Is last Sunday's bulletin available? What impression would a stranger get from reading the bulletin?

Go back outside. How would you know where to go if you were looking for the parish office? Is there a sign and can it be read from the street? If you were not from the parish, would you know which building the office is in?

Churches have sometimes unknowingly made it very difficult to find the parish office. Most Catholics have the idea that the parish office will be found right next to the church, usually in the rectory, and at one time, this was true. But lately, some priests have chosen to move their living quarters away from the church. The old rectory might still be the location for the parish office, but not necessarily. Sometimes the offices are found in a vacant convent or school, or another building on the church property. In some instances, the parish has purchased a different building or even a house down the street to use as the church office. When this is the case, it can be difficult to find the office if you are not a member of the parish (or even if you are a parishioner but have not paid attention to the changes).

The main point of this discussion is signs. What signs

invite someone to your parish and make them feel welcome? How would you feel if you were invited to someone's home for dinner, and when you arrived you found no lights on, the number of the house hidden, and no signs of life? Surely you would wonder about how welcome you really are.

The same is true of the parish. The church, the grounds, and the surrounding buildings should have an inviting look. The parish should present itself to the community as a place where people are not afraid to ring the bell or knock on the door. And this has as much to do with its appearance as it does with the people who make up the parish.

Very little about the appearance of a parish has to do with money, either: we're talking more about attention to detail. Your parish may be very wealthy, or it may be a community that wonders where the money for the electric bill will come from (most likely, it's somewhere in between). No matter what your resources are, the church reflects the concern and involvement of its community by the way it appears to others.

First impressions are lasting. What kind of first impression does your parish give? Every question raised about impressions requires some attention to detail: signs, plantings, sweeping, dusting, care in what is written about the parish. If you want to be user-friendly, you have to have a friendly look. It takes time and care but it is well worth it.

What happens when the sun goes down?

Let's talk about approaching the parish at night. Have you ever gone to a parish meeting only to find out that you could not *find* the parish meeting? Check your church bulletin announcements about meetings. When it says, "the Parish Pastoral Council will meet at 7:30 P.M. on Tuesday," does it say exactly where the meeting will be held? If your parish has a parish center or school, is the room where the meeting will be held identified? If the meeting is somewhere else, are adequate directions given? You cannot expect people to attend a meeting if they cannot find its location.

What about lighting? Where are the outdoor lights–if any–located? Evening meetings are terrible to attend when the parking lot is dark, the buildings are in darkness, and the one light that can be seen is in a room which you have no idea how to get to. Make sure that the parking area is lit and an outside light is on the building.

Also, see that an entrance door is open near to the meeting room. (Many of us have had the experience of walking completely around a building before finding the one open door.) I know security can be a problem, but there is a solution. Have someone from the group wait at the door to welcome and direct people. If the door has to be closed and locked once the meeting begins, so be it. (Of course, a couple of minutes for latecomers is always appreciated.) Another approach is to have the meeting in a room close to the entrance so that you can watch the entryway.

As society changes so too must the parish. Sad to say, it is often no longer safe for people to walk around the vicinity of the church at night. Although crime is on the decline in some areas, it is on the rise in others, and people may be afraid to come out at night alone. What can the parish do? Lights, lights, lights! Technology has made it possible to have lights which respond to movement, and some parishes have invested in motion-sensitive lighting. These types of lights are also a big help in parking lots.

It is helpful to trim overgrown hedges and clear walkways. Gestures such as these show concern for the safety of people and can encourage them to come together and participate more frequently.

Now I have one more question: Did you find anything unusual in this chapter? Just about everything I've suggested here is a simple way to appear welcoming and user-friendly. As a parish, you want people to be able to find you. Signs—signs of life, directional signs, signs of care, and the like—are essential to being a welcoming community. What do people see when they come to *your* parish?

QUESTIONS FOR REFLECTION

1. Drive up to your parish when you are not expected. What do you find?

2. Examine all the signs: are they clear? Well placed?

3. Go to the parish at night: check the lighting of doorways, walkways, and the parking lot.

4. Where is the parish office? Is it easy to find?

5. How does the parish's physical plant look? Can the appearance be improved?

6. Are there plants and flowers around the building? Should there be?

7. If improvements need to be made, who will do it? How much money can be allowed for this? Do you know who to contact?

CHAPTER TWO

Becoming a Welcoming Parish

Now that you have located your parish and considered its appearance, let's examine its welcome. When someone comes to the front door, who answers it? What do they say? Do you have an entry that is open or are visitors buzzed in? What is the tone of voice of the person who asks, "Who is it?"

I once arrived at a parish where I was expected for a meeting. When I rang the bell, a voice out of nowhere said, "What do you want?" in a tone which conveyed "Who do you think you are and what are you doing here?" Do you think I felt welcome? You guessed it!

I mentioned this treatment to the pastor and told him

how unwelcome I felt coming to his parish. I suggested that sometime he might want to walk up to the door, ring the bell, and see what happens when a stranger comes to his parish.

About a week later I received a phone call from the pastor, who told me he had done what I suggested. He relayed how shocked he was at what happened (he, too, was greeted in a rude manner). When he spoke to the secretary and asked why she sounded so abrupt, she told him that the doorbell was a regular interruption.

Yes, that it is. But our job *is* to be interrupted if we are the first voice someone hears on coming to the parish. Without people—and it is usually people who cause interruptions—we wouldn't have a parish, would we?

In discussing the situation with me later, this pastor realized he had the wrong person as the greeter. He wanted to make people feel welcome when they came to the parish, and so he did something about it by hiring a friendlier receptionist.

When the scenario with a rude receptionist was repeated at another parish, I mentioned to the pastor that I thought he should look into what was happening at his front door. He laughed and said, "Oh, that's just Barbara. She's always like that." So I asked him if he had any idea how many people may have walked away from the parish office when they heard her growl. He was so accustomed to this woman's cross personality that it took some convincing for him to understand that not everyone knows "how Barbara is." She was the first voice a stranger encountered at the parish office, and he agreed it was not a friendly voice.

These examples may be extreme, but they are both real. Have you ever checked to see how strangers are really greeted at your parish? Try it and find out.

Voice mail: blessing or curse?

Who answers the telephone at your parish? Because of modern technology, I should probably ask *what* answers the phone, as many parishes now have electronic answering systems.

Does this sound familiar? "You have reached St. Augustine Parish. No one is available to take your call, but if you leave a message, someone will get back to you as soon as possible. If you have a touch tone phone press one now: For Fr. Brown, press two; for the parish secretary, press three; for deacon Charles press four; all other calls, press zero. If this is a pastoral emergency, call our pager number, 367-9978."

Voice mail can be both a blessing and a curse. It helps people to keep in touch and can make communication more efficient. But contrary to what the communications industry salespeople would like you to think, many adults are not comfortable with the new communications technology.

Some people hang up as soon as they realize a machine is answering the phone. (They are the losers in this case because when voice mail is used properly, people do get in touch with each other more directly and immediately.) Other people do not wait to listen to the instructions. Like all technology, voice mail is only as good as the people who program and control it. Who controls the voice mail at your parish?

Perhaps a more basic question is this: Why does a parish have voice mail? Well, for one thing, voice mail enables the parish staff to be personally present to the people in front of them while still receiving telephone calls. It allows the staff to visit people in the parish and not miss any phone calls. It can also be a matter of economics: no one has to sit by the phone waiting for it to ring.

Voice mail makes it possible for parishioners and others to leave messages and know that the calls will be returned.

It can answer the most routine questions a parish office receives, including the Mass schedule. But all of this is true *only* if voice mail is actually used the way it was intended to be used.

Does a parish still need a secretary if it has voice mail? Most likely, the answer will be "yes" as there are many other things the parish secretary does besides answer the phone. What voice mail does for the secretary is allow her or him to answer the door and be present to those who come to the office. He or she does not have to say, "Wait a minute, please, I have to answer the phone." The visitor or staff member is treated more personably because the phone is being taken care of by the machine.

The parish secretary is not the only person voice mail helps. Each member of the staff can have someone in their office and know they are not missing phone calls. They can give their undivided attention to the person in front of them; and when they return phone calls, they can give their undivided attention to the person on the phone.

Voice mail is not magic. It only works if it is used properly. I was made painfully aware of this while at a conference recently. I had left a message on my voice mail saying that I would be out of the office for several days and would return phone calls when I returned. Even though I left a clear and explicit message, some people left messages assuming I would return their call within a couple of hours.

Before a parish begins to use voice mail, there should be some instruction given to the parishioners on when the system will go into operation and how it will work. A brief announcement can be made at Mass for several Sundays in advance. Step-by-step directions can appear in a small box in the bulletin which people can cut out and keep near their home telephone. If your parish sends mailings to parishioners' homes, a notice concerning the new phone system and how it works can be included in a mailing.

In regard to the actual use of the system, there are also some things which should always be done:

1) The outgoing message must be clear and changed regularly. The Sunday Mass schedule should not be the first thing a caller hears on Monday through Friday; this does not give anyone confidence that their call will be returned in a timely manner or that anyone pays attention to the messages.

2) Messages left on voice mail should be responded to as soon as possible. If a member of the staff is away, the outgoing message should indicate when the caller can expect a return call. When possible, it is also helpful to leave the number of someone to call in one's absence. Each staff person should be diligent in checking for messages and in returning phone calls. It is a matter of pastoral responsibility.

3) Sometimes power failures or human error erase messages. (This is not a usual occurrence and should not be used as an excuse for not returning phone calls.) Let parishioners know that if their call is not returned in a reasonable amount of time, please call again. Actually, if a power failure occurs in a particular week, a simple announcement can be made the following Sunday. This reinforces the fact that the staff is interested in communicating with the parish and acknowledges the limits of the technology at the same time.

4) Most parishes give an additional number to call if there is an emergency or the caller needs immediate help. Spend some time giving careful consideration to what number would be best to give here; be sure it is a number where someone (like the pastor, deacon, or pastoral associate) can be reached in a timely manner.

As I said earlier, voice mail is not magic: it does not solve all the communication problems of a parish. It is a useful tool and when used properly can save time and help the parish staff to be more present to parishioners and to each other. But it cannot solve all communications problems. People must still talk to other people with kindness. People must still exercise responsible judgment. People cannot fail in their pastoral responsibilities, neglect their duties, and say to themselves, "Oh, well, I have voice mail so I will eventually get those messages." We should never use voice mail as an excuse for not doing our job.

Voice mail can be the friendly first voice of the parish. Is this how it is used at your parish? If not, what needs to be changed?

Keep in touch

Everyone does not have voice mail or an electronic answering system. If you have someone who answers the phone regularly, think about these questions. What do they say when they answer the phone? How do they sound? What does their manner tell people about the staff?

Courtesy, kindness, and accurate information are essential for the person answering the phone. But each member of the staff has a responsibility to give the person answering the phone information about their whereabouts. Have you ever asked when a particular staff member might be available and been told, "I don't have any idea when I'll see her or him again"? Does this give you confidence in the effectiveness of the parish staff?

It doesn't take much time for a staff member to say, "You can tell anyone who calls that I will be in my office at such and such a time, and will be returning calls then." Or, "I will be at meetings all day and will return calls tomorrow unless it is an emergency." If staff people want to be responsive, this is the kind of information they should give to the greeter. They make it possible for the person answering the phone to do their job well and to be an accurate and welcoming voice on the phone.

A parish should be a place of collaboration and collegiality. The way a visitor—whether in person or on the phone—is greeted reflects greatly on the spirit of welcome in the parish. Take time to find out how people are welcomed in your parish.

What about special needs?

How user-friendly is your building to those who are physically challenged? Do wheelchairs fit through any or most doors in the church? The parish hall? The bathroom facilities? Where do people in wheelchairs fit into the body of the church? Are they in a space where they can fully participate in the liturgy or do they seem "in the way"? Some churches have moved out a pew or several half rows of pews so that people in wheelchairs can fit into the congregation and not feel out of place. This is being user-friendly.

How does your parish accommodate people who have difficulty hearing? Does your sound system reach to all corners of the church? Do you have a hearing loop system for the people who have a telecoil in their hearing aids? Are there people in the parish who know sign language and can interpret for those who need this?

The truly user-friendly parish welcomes all people by preparing ahead, by letting the congregation know that the facility is welcoming to the physically challenged. No user-friendly parish waits for laws to force them to be open to people who are challenged in any way.

QUESTIONS FOR REFLECTION

1. Is the parish office located in a place that is accessible to visitors? If not, are there ways to make it easier to get there?

2. Who answers the door and how do they do it?

3. How far do you have to go into the office before you actually meet anyone? When you see the first person, what do they say to you?

4. What kind of phone system does the parish have?

5. How many choices do you have if there is voice mail? Is it easy to use, or are callers likely to hang up in frustration?

6. Are staff messages answered promptly?

7. What kind of backup system do you have for callers?

8. If the office is locked and the greeting is poor, what can you do about it? Who can help remedy this?

9. Is your church accessible to people in wheelchairs?

10. Do you have sign language interpreters for the deaf? A hearing loop system, if needed?

11. If your facility is not open to those who are physically challenged in some way, what can be done about this?

CHAPTER THREE

Invitation to Liturgy

A smiling face, an outstretched hand, a cheerful voice which says, "Welcome to St. Augustine's...": this is a familiar sight for many parishioners today. Is this the welcome that people receive at your parish? Who is at the door as people arrive for Mass? Is anyone?

Is the welcome you receive at your church on Sunday any different from the welcome you receive at the local Wal-Mart or any of the new stores with this approach? I know a teenager who is very put off by the greeters at church: "It feels like Wal-Mart! All that is missing on the greeters is the uniform!" (I hesitated to tell this young woman that at some parishes the greeters *do* wear a special parish blazer or some other type of "uniform.")

What is the purpose of all this greeting? And if you don't have greeters at the doors of the church on Sunday, should you?

The point of a greeter is to make people feel welcome. But we need to ask a question here: do two or more greeters at the door of the church make a person feel welcome, or is it more due to a general atmosphere of welcome? Here's a more challenging question: does the Christian community relieve itself of its responsibility by appointing people to be at the door? If so, then the rest of us can simply come in, find a seat, and wait for the liturgy to begin.

I may be of a minority opinion on this, but I do not believe that the job of welcome can be given to a small group of people. Either we as a parish are a welcoming community or we are not. A couple of "glad hands" at the door does not excuse the rest of us from creating a climate where people feel welcome. Each of us has an obligation to smile at whoever comes into our pew, or at least acknowledge their presence with a nod of the head.

We may even have to welcome people by moving over and letting them share our pew! How many times have you walked down the aisle and found a whole empty pew with a "guard" kneeling or sitting at the end? That person sits with head bowed down, and ignores the fact that you have three children (or perhaps it is *because* you have three children). He or she lets you know by body language that you had better pick another place to sit.

When was the last time anyone in your church suggested that people move to the center of the pew to make room for others? Or if people need to sit at the end of the pew for some reason, that they move out of the way to allow someone else into the pew when someone comes by looking for a seat? We could be reminded in the bulletin or in a friendly sermon of the need to show welcoming by not guarding pew space. This is a very simple act that makes people feel welcome, when they can easily find a place to sit and see that someone has smiled at them.

There are many attitudes present in most of our congregations in regard to welcoming committees and greeters. One is to say, "Let them do it," and I can sit in my pew and feel smug that it's not my job. Or I can say, "Who cares if anyone feels welcome? That's not why people come to church, anyway."

Greeting and welcoming can take many forms. In our parish, a newly assigned priest asked people at the beginning of the liturgy to turn to their neighbor and welcome them, or introduce themselves if we did not know them. We have a very large parish and in the summer there are many visitors, so this was a good way to make people feel a bit more comfortable with each other. (It would be even better if we do this type of welcoming activity before Mass without being asked! Of course this would require some education of the community and acceptance of the fact that people make a difference.)

When we turned to our neighbors and greeted them, some people thought that the priest had moved the sign of peace to the beginning of Mass; they were surprised after the Our Father when the deacon instructed them to "turn to each other and offer a sign of peace." But the greeting at the beginning of liturgy had a different purpose, and it might have been wise for the priest to have taken a moment or two at the beginning of the Mass to explain this.

The priest might have emphasized the importance of the assembly and its role in celebrating the Mass, and how welcoming each other fits into that role. He then might have mentioned that this action was different from the sign of peace. All in all, however, the fact that we had two opportunities to communicate with our neighbor made us a very welcoming community that day!

Resistance to change

In some of our churches, this spirit of welcome is unheard of. "People come to church to talk to God, not their neighbor." This attitude speaks of a theology of individualism, a "me and God" approach. It completely leaves out the incarnational aspect of our faith and the social dimension of the Eucharist. The church is a community of believers, and Mass is our time to worship as a community.

"All that talking takes up too much time." This is another attitude that seems to be prevalent. My question is, why do people come to the liturgy, then? Are we so much into the fast-food, quickie-lube mentality that we can't even feel good about spending some extra time building community? How much time are we willing to give to God?

The Second Vatican Council emphasized the idea that we are the people of God; the church is a collaborative and collegial entity. As parish staff and lay ministers, we sell people short when we fail to introduce them to new ways of being church, new ways of acting out their belief in the incarnation. It is a golden moment of religious education and formation for the whole church when the time is taken to explain why we do what we do.

Are cold, unwelcoming communities more "holy" than those who meet, greet, share, and smile at each other? Some people might say yes. There are those who believe that a silent liturgy is more "holy" than one with verbal responses and singing. There are also people who believe that there should be silence at the beginning of Mass, out of respect for the "house of God." But a church is a house of the people of

God, of the people who make up the church. God loves us when we gather as a community to pray with and greet one another as much as God loves us when we are alone and silent.

The Document on the Liturgy written during Vatican II calls for "full, conscious, and active participation." The entire congregation needs to be formed in faith to understand what that means. The beginning of this process is greeting one another and being made welcome.

How welcoming is the community where you worship? What could be done to make it more welcoming? Are you willing to take the time to do what is needed?

QUESTIONS FOR REFLECTION

1. Does your parish have greeters? Are they friendly?

2. Are the people in your parish encouraged to speak with each other before Mass begins?

3. When was the last time you heard a homily about being a welcoming community?

4. Does your celebrant greet people before and after the liturgy? Why? Why not?

5. What instruction, if any, is available to parishioners who want to know more about the role of the assembly in liturgy?

6. Reflect on three ways that your parish is already welcoming people as they come to Sunday liturgy. Then, think of three other ways that your parish can make people feel more welcome.

CHAPTER FOUR

The Parish Staff: Who Does What?

Who makes up the parish staff? How do the people of the parish know who these people are and what they do? Here are the way three different parish bulletins in the diocese of Rochester, New York, list the people on the staff.

St. Mary's Church, Canandaigua, NY

Rev. Walter L. Wainwright, Pastor
Rev. Brian C. Cool, Parochial Vicar
Rev. Emmett J. Halloran, in residence
Mrs. Monette Mahoney, Director of Faith Formation
Mrs. Bonnie Keaveny, Parish Council Chairperson

Ms. Trixie Meteyer, Organist
Mrs. Eileen O'Neill, School Principal
Mrs. Patricia Simmons, Business Manager and Bookkeeper
Mrs. Dolores Finewood, Secretary
Mr. Rich Clayton, Maintenance Supervisor

St. Louis Church, Pittsford, NY

Rev. James A. Schwartz, Pastor
Rev. Kip Corriveau, Priest Intern
Deacon Thomas J. Driscoll, Minister of Christian Formation
Sr. Judith Ann Kenrick, RSM, Pastoral Associate
Stephanie Honz, Director of Liturgical Music
Lynne Boucher, Youth Minister
Kathleen Carroll, School Principal
Gail DeVoria, Religious Education Administrator
Lisa Magguilli, Chair, Parish Council
Sally Schrecker, Operations Manager
Birdie Proctor, Secretary and Bookkeeper
In Residence: Rev. John A. Reddington, Rev. James F. Slattery, and Mr. Jack Balinsky

Our Lady Queen of Peace, Rochester, NY

Rev. Dr. Joseph A. Hart, Pastor
Albert P. Bergeron, Deacon
Sr. Jacqulyn Reichart, RSM, Senior Pastoral Associate
Frank Henwood, Religious Education Administrator
Peter Wozny, Youth Minister
Verna Snyder, Parish Secretary
Beth Watkins, Religious Education Secretary
Esther Whelehan, Parish Bookkeeper

As you can see, the staffs vary in size for each of these parishes. What you will also notice is the difference in titles for the people who work for the parish. All three of these parishes have religious education programs but in each parish the person in charge has a different title and job description. One parish has a Religious Education Administrator, another has a Director of Faith Formation, and the third has a Minister of Christian Formation. One of the people in this position is a deacon, another is a religious woman, and the third is a layperson.

Do you know what each of these people does from the job titles listed in the bulletin? Do you think you could pass a test on what each of the job descriptions might entail? Probably not.

In any parish in the United States (or the world, for that matter), it would be difficult to know what a staff person does by reading the list on the front or inside the church bulletin. Different titles are used in different parishes for the same type of work. Without training, or a listing from the diocesan office of job titles and what they mean, it can be impossible to really know what a particular staff member does. Even then, each parish usually defines and refines the particular job a person has to do: no two job descriptions in two parishes are exactly the same.

If you have ever had a church job description, you also know that many things a person does are not found in the job description. In fact, many parish staff job descriptions have a catch-all phrase which reads something like this: "...and anything else required by the supervisor."

Why even talk about the staff and their responsibilities in the user-friendly parish? First of all, since we—the parishioners, through our weekly donations—pay their salaries, we should know what they do. Second, we should benefit from what the parish staff members do, or know who benefits, and how, from the work that is done. Third, we should be sure that what is being done is quality work by prepared people who know what they are doing. In the interest of common sense and good ministry, we should want to know that we are "getting our money's worth!"

I do not believe that each member of the parish has to have the same amount of information about what each person on the staff does. But I *do* believe that there are parishioners who should know exactly what each member of the parish staff does. These people would include the parish or pastoral council, the finance committee, and the trustees of a parish.

Who makes up the staff?

The number of staff members needed by a particular parish is largely determined by the size and location of the parish, as well as by its resources. Most parishes determine their staff membership by assessing the needs of the parish. If you have a religious education program in the parish, you will need someone to run the program. Then you must determine who else will be needed to help run the program: assistants, catechists, teaching helpers, and the like. Who will be paid, if anyone? Who is a volunteer? All of these are decisions that must be made by the pastor and his advisors.

In this process, the pastor or pastoral coordinator and other key people should come together to determine what are the staffing needs of the parish and how they are to be met. Also, staff members cost money, and money needs to be raised by the parish to cover the salary and benefits. This is a serious pastoral responsibility.

The cost of paying a just living wage has become an issue for parishes, especially parishes with limited incomes and many needs. This must be faced when hiring people to work for the parish, and it must be faced by the whole diocese if it means that in some parishes people's needs will not be met because of a lack of funds to pay professionally prepared, competent ministers.

In the user-friendly parish, the people of the parish play a significant role in the selection and ongoing evaluation of the staff. If the diocese has a personnel department, then the parish can use this office as a clearing house for suitable candidates which may be provided by that office. Still, the role of the pastor and the parishioners in determining the staffing needs of the individual parish is key.

Often when there is a change of pastor, there is upheaval on the staff. The assignment of the new pastor can affect how many of the old staff will remain in their jobs and how many will have to be replaced. No one should be surprised by this reality. Because running a parish is as much a business as any other, when the boss changes, the people who report to that person have to decide if they want to continue with the new administrator.

Canon law requires that a parish have a finance committee. Beside this obvious mandate, a pastor is smart to have such a committee simply because there are great advantages to having others consult and advise on financial decisions which the pastor must make on behalf of the parish. If the pastor wants to be free to do ministry, he would be wise to have a business manager, as well. Once again, the size of the parish and the skill of the pastor may indicate that only a part-time person is necessary. Wisdom dictates that the pastor do what he must to be accountable to the people and honest in the use of the money contributed.

There is also the business of fund-raising for the parish. In this day and age, a parish may have to compete for money in the same way that any charitable organization would. Though not something we like to think about often, fund-raising is essential not just to the mission of the parish but to the success of the programs. If you want to help the poor, you need money. If you want to pay just wages, you need money. For most of the priorities in any given parish, money is needed.

How do you get money? Basically, you have to ask for it. The pastor can make an appeal for money from the pulpit, and in many cases this is extremely effective. But for other parishes the best way to raise money is to use the help of a director of development, and to organize a parish stewardship committee. You can contact the diocesan finance office or the development office for their recommendations on someone who can help in this work.

Perhaps there is someone in the parish who has recently retired from a job that involved the skills necessary for fundraising. You might call on that person for advice. People who are retired or on the verge of retirement are often willing to lend their expertise to the parish, and can offer consultation in matters of contributions and stewardship.

Professional leadership: a given

As the number of clergy available for full-time parish work diminishes, the question of professionally trained pastoral ministers comes to the fore. Recent studies have shown that the "who" of ministry is not as important as "how" ministry is done. Where deacons, religious, and laypersons have been appointed to lead parishes in the absence of a priest, the questions of professional training are highlighted: not just any minister will do. The parish must be very selective in choosing someone who is competent and professionally prepared.

Most Catholics have come into contact with competent, compassionate ministers, be they clergy, religious, or lay. But the opposite is true, as well. All of us have known or experienced ministers who were less than effective in their work. In finding someone to lead a parish, the choice should be made of who is in sync with the parish, someone who can win the respect of the people because of their training and expertise as well as their personality. The psychological profile and the personal gifts of a potential parish leader should be considered, as well (although this can be a very touchy area).

The criteria for choosing a leader is key in the user-friendly parish. Faithfulness to the gospel and ethical living are important but cannot be the sole criteria when looking at public leadership. There is an argument which can be made for finding a suitable candidate in the community and preparing that person for leadership. But simple knowledge of the community and being a good person are not enough. Being a good person may be fine for running the parish festival and serving on a committee; even then, leadership skills, the ability to organize, and other charisms are often needed. The lifelong faith formation of our parish community is too important to leave to enthusiastic leaders with no theological education and grounding in the tradition.

Yes, professionals *are* needed to lead parish communities no matter what the parish's size, financial condition, or location. If there is one task that the diocese cannot ignore, it is the assurance that each and every faith community will have a competent, compassionate leader.

The ability of the parish to pay a just wage is really the overall task of the diocesan administration, as well. People who give their life to the church and who are willing to lead should be compensated for their work. All of our church documents support this, and finance committees need to be educated to this task. In the user-friendly parish, it should be a given that ministry is worth the cost.

QUESTIONS FOR REFLECTION

1. Do you know who is on your parish staff? List their names and job titles. Do you know what each person does?

2. Are there competent professionals who head key areas of ministry in your parish? If not, why not?

3. How are staff members replaced?

4. During your time in the parish, have you seen the staff increase or decrease? Why?

5. If the staff has decreased, was it for ministerial or financial reasons? If the decrease was for financial reasons, was the parish consulted? How?

6. How is fund-raising dealt with in your parish? Do you have an active stewardship program or committee?

7. Is there an opportunity for parishioners to have input on the parish staff? What avenues are open to parishioners who are concerned either about the size or the competence of the parish staff?

CHAPTER FIVE

The Parishioners: Who Does What?

In the last chapter, we looked at the staff and what they do. Now let's look at what the parishioners do in the user-friendly parish.

Take out a pen and paper or sit at your computer. Make a list of all of the activities under the heading "parish organizations." How many did you come up with? Do you know how many people are involved in each of these enterprises? No? I'm not surprised. It is my theory that no one knows. Not the pastor, not the director of religious education, not even the parish secretary (although it often seems that the secretary knows more than anyone else about what goes on in a parish).

Most likely, no one on the staff or in the parish has all the information about who is doing what for the parish. It is possible and probable that only God knows...and that's OK! What *should* you know? Here are some key questions about parish committees that the pastor and staff should have the answer to:

- What is the name of the committee?

- What is the purpose of the committee?

- Who is on the committee? (List the names.)

- When does the committee meet? Where?

- What are two significant things that this committee did last year?

- Is the work done by the committee still needed by the parish?

You may say, why should the parish staff know all this? First of all, nothing that is sponsored by the parish should be unknown to someone on the staff, if for no other reason than legal ramifications. If anything ever happened to anyone in the group while they were performing work for the parish, or even meeting on parish property, the parish could be liable.

A better reason to know who is doing what is so that the staff can be aware of what is important to its parishioners, what needs are being met in the community, and what should be done if there are needs not being met. Maintaining an open line of communication between the parish staff and the various parish groups can facilitate the spirit of collaboration and collegiality encouraged by Vatican II. It can also eliminate any duplication of effort.

Some parish pastoral councils begin a new council year by sharing information about each of the groups and/or committees in the parish. Ahead of time, a council member can ask each parish group or committee to prepare a handout or a large sheet of newsprint on which the following is written: a) the name of the group; b) who the members are; c) the goal or purpose of the group or committee; d) what are the significant events sponsored by this group; e) one event or activity from the last calendar year that the group is especially proud of; and f) goals for the coming year.

At the council meeting distribute the handouts, or post the sheets of newsprint around the room Allow time for everyone to read what has been written. You may want to have someone from each group or committee at the council meeting to elaborate on the written information, or to simply be available for questions.

When everyone on the council has had a chance to read the information, the council chairperson can ask everyone to look again at the various lists and see if they notice any duplication of purpose or activity between the groups or committees. You may also want to talk about whether there is a continued need for all of the groups or committees to exist or whether it might make sense to combine groups with similar purposes. This is especially true if, over the years, groups have come into existence to meet a specific need and never disbanded once that need was met.

If there is no redundancy, the council can proceed to discuss how they can assist each group to accomplish its goals for the following year. If overlapping responsibilities or activities are discovered, this is the time to discuss how this can be resolved. This kind of activity may be a revelation to the parish council by showing its members how many groups actually meet under the auspices of the parish. It also offers an excellent opportunity to consider how well the needs of the parish are being met by its groups and committees.

Committees

According the *Oxford American Dictionary*, a committee is "a group of people appointed to attend to special business." In the user-friendly parish, each committee has a purpose. The committee functions smoothly most of the time, and the meetings are well attended. At each meeting, the members know why they are there; when they leave, they know what they have to do before the committee meets again.

In the user-friendly parish, the committee structure is responsive to what the parish has identified as needs to be met. What committees does the parish need? The answer is connected to the goals of the parish. (If you have no goals for the parish, you may find it very difficult to know what kind of committees you need.)

Some kind of leadership group is essential, whether it is called the parish pastoral council, the leadership team, or whatever other name your parish chooses. What you want to be sure of is that it is *the* leadership group, and all other groups in the parish are somehow related to it. For clarity of purpose, this group is the one that oversees the other groups or committees. This group sets the vision and keeps the other groups focused.

One system which seems to work for some parishes is to have all of the groups meet on the same night. (This has another practical advantage, that is, it ensures that you do not have the same people on all the committees.) If there are any questions for the pastoral council, all the people have to do is walk across the room. The parishes that I have seen which use this model seem to like it, and it appears to be an efficient way to do business. The principle of subsidiarity is lived out in a system such as this, when the decisions are made at the lowest level possible. The pastoral council lets the committees do their work.

In most of the parishes I have worked with, there are usually at least four other committees. These are: liturgy, finance, education, and social action. Some parishes have a separate parish life committee, and others have parish life activities which originate from each of the committees at different times of the year. Each parish should reflect on its constituency and resources and decide how to organize.

There is an even more radical idea that could occur depending on the professional training of the parish staff. In a user-friendly parish with a highly trained staff it might be possible to have no standing committees. All work would be done on an ad hoc basis. This could be a way to proceed if there is a full-time parish staff, and if the commitment level of the parishioners tends to burn out quickly.

One advantage of working this way is that more people can be involved with less time commitment. When you volunteer to work with a group or committee, you are not volunteering for life but for a limited period of time. The staff has to work harder with this process, but energized, dedicated professionals could find this a more creative approach. The staff can develop new things as they go along and not be encumbered by a fixed structure that hinders rather than helps ministry. (Too-rigid structures have killed more creativity than any of us would care to admit.)

The down side of the ad hoc system is that it could be too loose an organization to be effective in the parish. Details can fall in the cracks, and plans which are executed may not receive the valuable follow-up that could benefit committees in the future.

The essential thing to remember in any organization is to

keep the end result in mind. There should be no group without a statement of purpose. When you have a purpose, you can achieve a goal; if you do not have a purpose, you will not know why you are gathering together, and the group will flounder.

Groups and committees should always set a term of office so that a member can stop doing the work without dying or moving out of the parish. It is also helpful to have some system of evaluation in place to know whether a group is operating effectively, and whether changes need to be made.

Parishes are usually great at creating new groups to address needs; but they often have a hard time putting an end to a group once its purpose has been served. For example, think about a committee set up to wrap bandages for the American Revolution which is still in existence today. The people on the committee might like each other and they may be doing some worthy work but we all know that they obviously are not wrapping bandages for the American Revolution.

A goal or purpose, dedicated members, regular meeting times with an agenda: all of this is required for legitimate committees. You should never attend a meeting without an agenda. And...if there is nothing to be done before the group meets again, you should question whether the group *should* meet again. Without an agenda and nothing to do, groups and committees lose their sense of purpose. Then, its members would do better staying home and bonding with the significant people in their lives.

Too often, we go to parish meetings out of a misplaced sense of obligation. If we are in a truly user-friendly parish, we will not find ourselves being "used" or "abused." To be at meetings with no purpose is a unique kind of ecclesial abuse. Do not engage in it or be a party to it.

Doing the work

In a user-friendly parish, the people who do the work are trained or taught how to do the work that is needed. From serving on the liturgy committee to running the coffee hour, if you are doing work in the parish, (hopefully) someone has helped you to learn what to do.

In the user-friendly parish, no one is just given a key and told, "go do this...." When a person volunteers to do any job, someone on the staff or someone who has done the job before should assist the new person to learn how to do the job. It is not by osmosis that someone learns how long it takes for a forty-cup coffee pot to perk, and how much coffee to put into it. I know people who have volunteered to run the coffee hour after Mass and have been told what time to arrive but nothing else...and sometimes, there is no one else there to help them when they do arrive.

In the user-friendly parish, this would never happen. People would be met, shown where the coffee pots are, told how long it takes for the pots to perk, and taught how to do everything that is needed. They would learn where all the supplies are kept, and the like. In the truly user-friendly parish, not only would someone be with you but cabinets would be marked with contents. A printed sheet would help the people to remember what needs to be done and in what order. When they have to do it a second time, it would be a lot easier and they would feel more confident.

When people volunteer for a job and are not told what to do for that job, frustration and embarrassment result. Rarely, if ever, do people who have found themselves in this position volunteer again. Then the people on the leadership team say such things as, "I don't understand why people won't volunteer for anything in this parish."

Committees are helpful to getting work done. There are

correct and incorrect ways of organizing people as well as inviting them to participate in the work. The goal of the user-friendly parish is to make serving both the people and the parish a relatively easy task, and not a difficult one. We want the people to serve with joy, not pain and frustration. Therefore, we need to put the structures into place and make the effort to ensure that this will happen.

QUESTIONS FOR REFLECTION

1. List the major groups and committees in your parish. Do you know what they do? If not, how can you find out?

2. Would you like to try the "no standing committees" model in your parish? Why or why not?

3. Have you ever volunteered to do anything in your parish? If so, were you taught how to do that job?

4. Have you ever been chair of a committee or head of a project? Did you train the people who helped you? Would you now?

5. Are the times of parish events convenient to the schedule of the people in your parish? If the answer is "no," can you do anything about it? How?

6. Are all the groups or committees of the parish serving a useful purpose? If not, how can this be remedied?

CHAPTER SIX

What Does It Cost to Belong?

When I was growing up in the city of New Orleans, there were money changers at the door of the church on Sunday morning. These men (and they were all men) stood watch over a table stacked with little towers of change, so that people coming to Mass could pay their "pew rent." At the time, this amounted to fifteen cents for each child and a quarter for each adult in the family.

Although this practice was discontinued years ago in all Catholic churches that I am aware of, parishioners are still expected to contribute to the church on a regular basis. What happens in your parish if a person consistently attends Mass and does not contribute? Do you know?

Have you ever sat in a pew with no money in your pocket on a Sunday morning, knowing that your weekly church envelope was sitting right on the counter at home where you left it when you rushed out the door to be on time for Mass? And how did you feel sitting there in the church with nothing to put in the basket as the usher came by? Most likely, you felt guilty. And why?

Because this is the scenario in many churches at collection time: the ushers walk up and down the aisles with the basket. At each pew they stop, shake the basket, and look each person in the eye before going on to the next pew. Now, if you have your envelope or some money to put in, you're fine. But if you don't...could a convicted prisoner on his or her way to jail feel more guilty than you did then?

You may say, "Hey, you should not feel guilty if you give regularly." Right! But can you control how you feel when you are confronted by the shaking basket, the piercing look? (Frankly, my first thought when this happens is to push the basket away and say, "I gave last week.")

Who trains the ushers in your parish? Are your ushers considered part of a welcoming committee and taught how to pass the collection basket without intimidation? Some parishes simply pass a basket up and down the aisles during the collection. This can be a better way, but the ushers still need to pass and collect the baskets, and should show discretion.

The leaders of the parish—including the pastor and the priests—should know what it is like to sit in the pews in their parish. If you are in a leadership position in the parish and have experienced what I am talking about, don't make a joke about it or call it an idiosyncrasy of a particular usher. Address the problem from the point of view of welcome and being made to feel a part of what goes on whether you are able to contribute on a certain Sunday or not.

Alternatives for the collection

There are parishes where a basket is never passed. At each entrance of the church, there is a box or a basket where parishioners can drop in their weekly donation as they come into or leave the church. Some churches have a permanent structure for a collection basket, where people drop in their offering before Mass. Then, at the preparation of gifts, the usher takes out the basket and brings it to the altar with the other gifts.

There is sometimes a special place designated for all donations, so that if a parish holds a food drive or other such collection of goods, these baskets are all found in one location. This approach encourages the community to bring their gifts as they begin the liturgy. Of course, people may forget to leave their offering on the way in, so they can do so on the way out. Visitors who may not be accustomed to this manner of collection can also leave their gifts on the way out.

Does the parish with the gift station at the door get more in donations or less? With appropriate education and time, there does not seem to be a significant difference in the amount collected between passing the basket and having a collection station at the door.

Some parishes have also taken advantage of modern banking practices, and have parishioners who designate the church as a payroll deduction. Other parishes accept credit card payments as a way of making a donation to the church. (This practice has become popular in some Catholic schools, as well.) Some people enjoy the convenience of contributing this way, while others would not think of using this method.

The most important consideration here is the role of the offering as it fits within the liturgy. The action of offering the gifts of the assembly should be seen as a liturgical action.

Whatever means of collection is used, the liturgical connection and the importance of stewardship should be obvious,
understood, and experienced by all present.

Why give?

Ultimately, how people contribute to the parish is not as
important as why they contribute. The key question here is:
who and what is being supported by the weekly donations
to the church?

Research studies on church contributions show that
Catholics want to give to their parishes when they understand the need. If people believe their needs are being met
and they approve of the way their money is used, they continue to give. Even in the poorest parishes, people will be
generous to the church when their needs are met. The issue
is rarely the generosity of the people: it is usually connected
to the mission of the church and whether the parishioners
perceive that the parish staff cares about them. How are the
people treated? What is the money used for? Is the parish
welcoming and attentive to its people? These are the questions which determine the level of giving.

I have been a member of parishes where the only men-
tion of money is in the annual financial report. The pastors
of these churches did not ever have to ask for money. The
church was full for Sunday Masses, the liturgies were uplift-
ing, the committees were energetic, and the collection basket full. There is nothing like a satisfied customer.

How much money is contributed to your parish on a regular basis? Do you know? Is a financial statement published
in the parish bulletin? Does your parish have a finance committee as required by canon law? If not, why not?

In the user-friendly parish it is understood that the money
collected is the people's money, and it is treated with

respect. The people are asked politely to contribute to the financial support of the parish, and they are kept informed about how the money is spent. It is the wise administrator who keeps account and is accountable to the people.

Time and talent

Financial contributions are not the only means of parish support. People give time and share their talent to build the kingdom of God where they live. Some parishes have attempted to quantify the number of people and hours given to the parish over a calendar year. Much to those churches' chagrin, it was almost impossible. The number of people who contribute their time to parish activities is nearly impossible to count, and the number of hours far more difficult.

But the truth is that a parish runs on a unique combination of the time, talent, and treasure of people who are committed to building the kingdom of God where they live. Some parishes have literally been built by the people. There are parishes where the original church has to be expanded and the building project was undertaken by the people of the parish. These people make a unique investment of time and talent to the parish.

In the user-friendly parish where the people in charge are creative, there are many different ways people can be connected to contribute to the health and development of the life of the parish. Homebound people can be called on to make phone calls for the parish. They can also become a unique support to each other with a telephone tree. Each one calls another one daily to say hello and chat for a while. The tree is changed periodically so that different people can talk to each other. Some parishes need to have their bulletins folded weekly, or envelopes stuffed for special mailings. This can be a great way to use the time and talent of homebound people, while keeping them involved in the life of the parish.

Another parish project might be to have teenagers babysit for the children of adults who wish to attend adult education classes or parish meetings. If programs for adults are held during the day, grandparents might be invited to act as babysitters so that parents who don't work outside the home during the day can participate. Another excellent intergenerational project is for a parish to get together with a group such as Habitat for Humanity and build a home.

Small communities of people with like needs and desires are the key to helping people connect. I know of one parish that started an "empty nest" group. On Sunday afternoon the parish invited all interested parents whose children had grown up and left home to come to the parish center; the planners were amazed at the number of "empty-nesters" who showed up. The parents spent time talking with one another, and eventually broke into groups based on common interests. Some people arranged to have dinner together, others decided to meet for a discussion after reading the same book, and a group interested in music planned to attend a concert together.

The user-friendly parish can provide opportunities for people to connect to one another. Let the interests and needs of the people be heard, and then facilitate the process of bringing these people together. You are only limited by your imagination.

If you don't give, can you still belong?

This is a key question for the leadership of the user-friendly parish. If a person never uses the weekly donation envelopes, can they still belong to the parish? If they are not involved in any of the parish activities, are they less of a member of the parish than those who are active?

Common sense does not serve us well here, because it would argue that without involvement, you are not a part of the group. But unlike other organizations and clubs, the parish should hold itself to a higher standard. There is an old saying that "there is no rock so hard that a little drop of water can't beat admittance in a thousand years." I know we don't have a thousand years but we do have time to be compassionate and welcoming to whoever comes to our church.

We can welcome people and be kind and inviting; when they are ready they will respond. We may never see their gifts but that does not mean they are not there. The worst thing a Christian community can do is make people feel unwelcome because they have no money to give, or choose not to give their money to the church, or not spend time on parish committees. This "exclusive" approach has been practiced before in our parishes, and it does not work. It is anti-gospel.

Look at the members of your parish, at the many people over the years who have kept the parish financially solvent, who have given countless hours of energy, wit, and wisdom. Your parish is what it is today because of all the people who have participated (or not) before. Our job in the user-friendly parish is to build the kingdom of God with the talent and resources available to us now. It is our responsibility to welcome all and judge no one. If we can travel this road with a light heart and happy expectations, we will be amazed at the response of the people.

In those parishes where money is never mentioned, it is usually because an attitude of welcome and care exists there. The bottom line is: do you, as a parish, want to be known for your fund-raising abilities, or do you want to be known for your open welcome, vibrant parish life, and compassionate treatment of all who come to you?

The user-friendly parish knows that the true gift of a Christian community is to live in hope and wait for people to respond in their own way. Respect and compassion go a lot farther than intimidation and tyranny in all things—but especially, in giving money to the church. Be a community that people want to belong to, and they *will* give generously of their time, talent, and treasure.

QUESTIONS FOR REFLECTION

1. What financial expectations does your parish have of its people? How do you know?

2. Besides the Sunday collection, what other means of donating money are available in your parish?

3. Are you satisfied with the way money is spent by your parish? Why? Why not? If you are not satisfied, what are you going to do about it?

4. Does your parish acknowledge gifts of time and talent? How?

5. Does your parish have activities and opportunities for people to connect to one another? If not, who could help you start this type of activity in the parish?

6. Are people treated differently if they do not contribute financially to your parish? Have you ever heard a homily or other talk which made you feel uncomfortable because you were not a "big giver?"

7. Do you have to belong to a committee or "do something" to be welcomed in your parish? If you answered "yes," do you think this is how things should be? Why or why not?

CHAPTER SEVEN

The Parish in
the Community
and in the World

The parish does not exist in a vacuum. It is part of a neighborhood, a city or town, a state, a country, and ultimately, the world. It is a thread in the fabric of society. The user-friendly parish should be a vital part of what goes on where it exists. This means that it is a known organization in its area, a part of what goes on around it. The members of the parish are integral to the life of the city or town where the parish exists.

One way the parish participates in the life of the area

where it is located is by encouraging the people of the parish to participate in the civic life of the community, from voting in local elections to serving on boards and volunteering for community-sponsored events. I know there are people who say that the church should not get involved in politics. But our society is governed by people in political office; decisions are made by people in office which affect the quality of life for all of us.

It is irresponsible, in my opinion, *not* to get involved in local politics. I will use a simple example: in one town, there was the possibility of setting up a group home for the disabled. Some of the citizens in the town were afraid that their property values would go down if the house was allocated to the disabled. This was irrational fear since there were other group homes in the town which had not negatively impacted the property values.

The pastor of the local parish preached about justice and fair housing for all people. He asked the people of the parish to become involved and make their wishes known to the elected officials. Some people in the parish were outraged. How could the pastor ask people to get engaged politically? The pastor's response to this was: "How could I not?" In the interest of justice, he felt that it was his obligation not just to preach justice but to do something about the violations of justice where he lived.

I know of another instance where a young cleric became a member of the local volunteer fire department. New to the area, it was a way for him to serve the community, but also a way to become known and trusted by the people of the town. Caring about a real concern gave this young man entry into people's lives that he might not otherwise have had. It was an effective ministry for him and his people.

Another area that is often overlooked by parishes is participation in the justice system. After I was on jury duty a few years ago, I wrote an article for *Today's Parish* magazine about that experience and the negative comments I heard from people about serving on the jury. If good people all say "No," who will serve? The user-friendly parish can make it possible for people in the parish to serve on jury duty by providing child care and other support services, especially for single parents who are called to serve.

The user-friendly parish encourages its members to be involved in signing petitions to recycle, to keep the air and water clean, to support honest officials, and encourage good people to sit on the zoning boards, town councils, and other committees whose work affects the environment.

Other areas of community service can include support for emergency squads and blood drives. Events which help these concerns are usually easy to organize by contacting the local Red Cross or hospital. And if your parish does not sponsor its own food bank or homeless shelter, find out what the needs are in your community and how your parish can participate.

Parishes should be "good citizens," and they do this by getting involved in the civic life of the community. If the parish ignores its responsibility to be engaged in helping this way, it is not user-friendly.

Support of the military and law enforcement

How does the user-friendly parish support the military? Our goal may be to work for peace, but many parishes have families who are engaged in military work. In recent years, the United States has been involved in "peacekeeping" activities where young men and women have been sent to foreign countries to protect the rights of others. What does the user-friendly parish do to support such people?

Ultimately, the purpose of those in military service is to protect the interests not only of our own country but of other countries who need our help and assistance. In the user-friendly parish, people involved in military work are treated with respect and occasionally thanked for the service they provide.

The same applies to those who work in law enforcement. How do the people in the parish support any public officials involved in law enforcement, the CIA, the FBI, or the local police? What kind of language is used in regard to these people? In the user-friendly parish, these men and women are treated with respect and honored on occasion, not just when they are needed.

When a crime is committed, the general populace is quick to call on the men and women in law enforcement positions. The user-friendly parish does not wait for crime to happen. The parish can engage in dialogue with law enforcement people to make the parishioners aware of how to protect themselves as well as things they can do to discourage criminals from coming into their homes. A user-friendly parish forms partnerships which are helpful to the people and realizes its place in the local community.

Being a global church

The user-friendly parish sees itself as part of world community, as well. As such, we have a responsibility to be aware of events around the globe and to do our part to ensure justice where and when it is needed. We may be called upon to ration items or boycott products produced by child labor. These are just two ways the user-friendly parish can exercise its role in the global community.

When a papal document is published, what is the response of the parish? Is it made aware of the documents?

When the National Conference of Catholic Bishops publishes a document or a video, how does the parish learn about the contents? What about your connection to your own diocese? Is your diocesan staff user-friendly? How do they distribute and explain documents from your diocesan office?

What is the moral obligation of the parish to the authority of the local bishop? What is the local bishop's relationship to the user-friendly parish? When is there interaction with the bishop? Is it only in time of crises? Do you invite your bishop to share your small victories and celebrations? Are you friendly to the bishop? Do the people in the parish know the bishop? Have they ever seen him when it was not confirmation time?

To paraphrase the popular adage, no parish is an island (even if it is located on one!). We are part of a bigger picture and should be aware of our connections and responsibilities. The people in the user-friendly parish must be good citizens of the neighborhood, town, city, state, nation, and the world. We want the user-friendly parish to know and exercise its relationship to the local church and diocese, to participate in consultations from the National Conference of Catholic Bishops, and to understand its relationship to the Holy Father.

Each of these relationships requires planning, involvement, reading, education, and acknowledgment of the unique aspects of the relationship. Our society needs gifts of time, talent, energy, and money. It also requests that we understand our place and exercise our rights and duties.

Community assistance

The work lives of many people have changed rapidly over the past decade. Companies all across the world have been involved in downsizing and corporate mergers. This means that many people who had thought their futures were secure have found themselves out of work.

Often, people have unemployment forms to fill out and they need help. What better service in a time of such need could the user-friendly parish provide? More than one parish is now involved in helping people who have been "de-selected" (a term used by the president of Kodak in alerting people that they no longer worked for the company) find new jobs or means of work. These parishes set up an ad hoc committee to facilitate applications and job requests. Companies who are in need of workers contact the committee to let them know of their needs and to send people to interview for the jobs that are available. Committee members also make connections with other businesses to seek out opportunities, and they provide references and clerical support for the unemployed when possible.

We are all aware of our financial responsibility to our country (especially when we look at our paycheck deductions). Does the parish encourage its people to be honest in paying their taxes? I know of a parish where volunteers assist people in filling out their tax forms. This parish has posted hours when people can receive help not only with tax forms, but with medical forms or other government forms. The people of the parish simply come to the parish center at the appointed times and know that someone will be there to help. This tremendously valuable service was originally set up to help the elderly but the parish soon discovered that this service was needed by all age groups.

Many towns and villages offer assistance with electric or heating bills in the winter for people who cannot afford to pay the full price. The user-friendly parish makes this information known and helps those who need it to apply. A simple way to do this is to publish all the telephone numbers of local service agencies each week in the church bulletin. Another approach is to have someone from the parish social action committee speak at the end of each liturgy on a given weekend and highlight the community help which is available to parishioners.

Parishes should also be aware of people in their neighborhood who are not members of the parish, but who may need help. If anyone knows of someone who is housebound or otherwise disabled, they could be contacted to see if the parish can help in any way. Rather than wait for people to come to them for help, parishioners should be aware that not everyone who needs help knows where to go or who to ask. This is truly the meaning of outreach, when we go out to those in the community to see what we can offer them. This is what a parish ought to be about, inclusive and caring for all in need.

I know there will be those who say, "We have enough to take care of on our own. We do not have enough volunteers to serve our own needs; why should we get involved in these other issues?" Yet if the parish is not aware of its connection and responsibility to the larger community, the larger church, and to the world, it is not engaged in building the kingdom of God. It is merely a self-serving entity, selfish and myopic. If this is the attitude of a parish, I would wonder if it is even Catholic.

QUESTIONS FOR REFLECTION

1. Do you believe that your parish should be involved in politics? Why or why not?

2. Has anyone in your parish ever encouraged the assembly to vote? To be involved politically?

3. Has your parish ever been involved in a neighbor-hood project sponsored by the town/city/village? Was it a good experience? Why? Why not?

4. If you answered "yes" to question three, do you think this kind of activity should be repeated?

5. Is support for the military something you have heard preached about in your church? If not, why do you think this is so? Should it be preached about?

6. Are law enforcement personnel visible in your congregation? Do they feel welcome?

7. What is the relationship between your pastor and the bishop of your diocese? Have you ever met your bishop?

8. Has the pope visited your diocese? Did you see him in person? Is he spoken of with respect in your parish?

9. If there was a major shift in the workforce where you live—for example, the closing of a major company—did your parish do anything to assist the displaced workers? What did they do? If nothing was done, why not?

10. Are you satisfied with the "citizenship" of your parish? If not, why? What will you do about it?

CHAPTER EIGHT

How Does the Parish Communicate?

How we communicate to parishioners and the greater community determines, in large part, the degree to which the parish will be of service to others. There are many ways for a parish to communicate with others: verbally, through homilies, classes, and people interaction; by written means, including the bulletin, e-mail, and letters; and by our actions within the parish and beyond. Let's look at a few of these vehicles.

Getting your message across

In most parishes, the church bulletin is the major means of communication. How user-friendly is your bulletin? Is the information in your bulletin clear and understandable, or is it like a message from the CIA to one of its operatives—in others words, cryptic? Messages in the parish bulletin may appear to be secret messages because you have to be "in the know" to understand them. Here is an example: "The CDA will meet in the CYO at seven on the seventeenth. Everyone is invited." What is the CDA, and where is the CYO? The seventeenth of what month? Everyone is invited? Are they serious? (What would they do if everyone came?) I think we would all agree that this is *not* a user-friendly notice.

What about announcements at the end of the liturgy on Sunday? Have you ever sat in the pew and wondered "What is she saying?" or "Who is that message for?" At the end of the announcements in some churches the presider always says, "Read the bulletin for this and other important messages." If you are going to read it in the bulletin anyway, why do we want to hear it?

As an interesting exercise, have someone outside the parish read your Sunday bulletin or newsletter and give you his or her opinion of what the parish says about itself there. Also, there are a lot of communication consultants around today, and it might be a good idea to ask one to evaluate your parish publications and public announcements for clarity of message and meaning.

Electronic equipment enables all kinds of things. One parish I know uses a computer and power point to display important messages on the wall of the church. These keep on repeating just like the electronic message boards in hotels and convention centers. Another parish uses an overhead with the words to the songs in large print on the walls next to the altar (remember "follow the bouncing ball" singing?). The advantage here is that there seems to be more congregational singing, if for no other reason than that everyone's head is looking up at the altar instead of being buried in a book.

The town crier

How do the people of your town know what your parish is doing? Do you send press releases about important events–or even just news about what's going on in the parish–to the local newspapers and TV/radio stations? Do you use the "free ads" available in the newsprint handouts that are often distributed locally? Does someone on the pastoral council or on the staff have the job of public relations for the parish? Are parishioners encouraged to act as ambassadors of the parish?

Communication about the parish–its goals, hopes, events, and the like–can be an effective way to reach out to persons who have removed themselves from the church. Are Christmas or the yearly parish mission the only times when you invite alienated members back to your parish? How do you communicate with these people? Helping everyone in the parish be aware of their role as an "inviter" is key to the mission of the church.

Most Catholics are aware of the diminishing number of clergy today. One response might be to look at the image we present as a parish, and as parish staff and committee members. Are we the kind of group a young person would look at and say "I'd like to be a part of that team…these are people that I would like to lead, and would enjoy working with"? We often have a "romantic" notion that a vocation is simply a call from God. But the reality is that it is also a serious career choice for a young person to make. Is our "workplace" appealing to a prospective "employee"?

How is the parish seen by those not related to it? Is it seen as a source of life and caring so that people not connected to the parish ask themselves, "Why don't *I* belong to a church like that?" Are the liturgies enlivening…homilies meaningful…people friendly and welcoming? How do non-parishioners regard the parish? Do the women in the beauty shop and the men at the local barber speak well of the parish and staff? Do people who are hired by the parish to fix the plumbing and electricity find friendly faces at the parish office? Do they see people being nice to each other as they go about their work?

In recent years, many young people (and adults) have begun to wear bracelets and other jewelry that read "WWJD." The letters stand for the question "What would Jesus do?" and remind wearers to ask themselves this question when they are stuck with making a decision. This is actually a good question for many of us to ask when it comes to issues of communication.

Jesus used a variety of ways to communicate with his disciples and followers, as well as with strangers and politicians. He gave us a good example in how to speak directly and clearly yet from the heart, always keeping God's word and will foremost in this regard. Jesus responded to fundamental questions with respect and charity, aware of each person's interests and intent.

Some people think it is a gift to be able to speak to different age groups and be understood by all. I think that it is a skill which anyone can learn if one is willing to take the time. Often, good communication is simply a matter of asking the audience "Is this clear?" "Do you understand?" or "What do you think?"

Means of communication

"Written" does not mean just paper and pen in this age of computers. If there are people in the parish who are competent and enjoy using computers, why not take advantage of this new way to communicate?

I know of a parish which regularly communicates by e-mail with parishioners who are away at college. Sometime in September, a call goes out for all the e-mail addresses. Then, at break time, before the holidays, or when something special is going on at the parish, an e-mail message goes out to all the students. The students in the parish have responded with great enthusiasm to this gesture which keeps them in touch with the parish and shows that their church cares about them. The pastor of this user-friendly parish is the first to admit that, although he does not know how to use a computer himself, electronic mail offers a wonderful opportunity to be welcoming and friendly to those away at school.

This particular parish also has another user-friendly idea to stay in touch with college students. Twice a year, at exam time, the parish sends a "care package"–energy bars, tea, hot chocolate, cookies, and the like–to those away at school. This too lets the students know that they are being thought of at an especially stressful time.

The user-friendly parish invests in its future by investing in its young people. Communicating both by word and deed shows that they care.

Outside communications

Do you place your bulletin in the local laundromat, the library, the fast food outlet, or the doctor's offices in your parish? Have you made any attempts to put your bulletin any place other than in the hands of your parishioners?

If you want to be an inviting parish, leaving your bulletin in unlikely places is a good way to reach people. You could even have a notice put in the bulletin which says, "If you are reading this for the first time, come worship with us next

Sunday!" You might be amazed by the response you receive. Put the bulletin in places where people have to wait. Is there a bus station or train station near your parish? Be clever but not obtrusive. One caveat: be sure you have permission to leave the bulletin in each location, as you do not want to generate bad will in any way.

A big part of communication is advertising. How do you let people know about the occasions and events which are coming up? Do you have a calendar that is public and updated? Where is the calendar published? Does everyone in charge of an activity know how to access the calendar? Some parishes have found it helpful to put a large weekly calendar on the wall at the major entrance of the church. One creative parish uses an overhead projector to display a large-sized bulletin on the wall of the vestibule at the end of each Mass on Sunday.

Many parishes publish a monthly calendar with changes noted in the Sunday bulletin. You may wonder why a church should have a monthly calendar if there are going to be changes. But new things do come up. Events occur which were not known about when the monthly calendar was printed. If nothing else comes out of this chapter or even this book, I hope you realize that in order to be user-friendly you have to be flexible and open to life as it happens. The worst mistakes are made when people feel that something can never be changed.

How much time do you want to spend to be sure that you are giving a clear message? What do you do to find out if the message you are giving is understood? How much money are you willing to invest in communication? These are the decisions you have to make. The result of your decision making should lead to a well-informed community.

QUESTIONS FOR REFLECTION

1. Who is responsible for the majority of communications in your parish? How was the person chosen?

2. Is communication satisfactory in your parish? If not, why not?

3. What is the major method used for communication in your parish?

4. Has your parish used e-mail or any other electronic means of communication? If not, why not?

5. Is your bulletin well written? If not, what are you going to do about it? By when?

6. How does your parish advertise itself and the events that occur there?

7. Do you know where the parish calendar is kept? Is it useful? Clearly written? How are changes noted?

10. If you wanted to put something on the parish calendar, would you know who to contact and how?

11. Does your parish have a Web page? If so, how is it used? If not, is this something that might be beneficial to parishioners?

CHAPTER NINE

Why Be User-Friendly?

Just then a lawyer stood up to test Jesus. "Teacher," he said, "what must I do to inherit eternal life?" He said to him, "What is written in the law? What do you read there?" He answered, "You shall love the Lord your God with all your heart, and with all your soul, and with all your strength, and with all your mind; and your neighbor as yourself." And he said to him, "You have given the right answer; do this, and you will live." Luke 10:25–28

Being a user-friendly parish means implementing the admonition found in the gospel passage above: love your neighbor as you love yourself. Attention to the appearance of the church; concern about how we welcome people; awareness of what we communicate to our community;

these are all practical manifestations of Christian love. It is the quiet kind of love in action that should mark each and every one of our parishes.

People may say, "Most parishioners come to church to fulfill their Sunday obligation; nothing else really matters to them." Yet it is false to assume that people come to Sunday liturgy only because they "have to." Studies have shown that most people come to church on Sunday because they want to be there. The majority of the people in our congregations are not there out of obligation but out of a desire to live a good life, to find nourishment for the spiritual journey, and to share the companionship of God and of their fellow Christians. Knowing this should make the desire to be a user-friendly parish a paramount concern.

Now that you know that people come to church because they want to be there, you should treat them better. What does this mean? In recent years, the Catholic parish has sometimes been criticized for its failure to be welcoming; non-Catholic churches have a reputation of being more welcoming. After attending a wedding or funeral at a non-Catholic church, many Catholics comment on the warm reception they receive there.

Try this experiment. For the next three Sundays, look at the people who sit around you at liturgy. You will find that most often the same people sit in the same pew week after week. If you have been going to this church for a while—and sitting in relatively the same place each week—wouldn't you think that you might know these people by name? Do you?

In an earlier chapter I described how in one church, after the opening song, the priest encouraged the people to introduce themselves to one another and to welcome strangers. Because this is a large parish, there was not much more than the opportunity to shake hands with a few people and say "hello." And perhaps that is all that is really necessary. But here's another example: on a recent trip to Canada, I went to a church where the congregation was much smaller. There the priest said, "Turn to your neighbor, say hello, introduce yourself and tell each other where the best place is to pick apples today." This interlude helped everyone there to relax, and allowed the liturgy to proceed in a more open and responsive manner.

From the first greeting of the liturgy to the final "Go in peace...," the people must be welcomed and encouraged.

Making the change

We would all agree that change can be difficult. If you want to implement any of the suggestions in this book, you have to practice patience, a virtue which can be very hard to come by. It is often easier to do something ourselves rather than wait for someone else to do it; but when we wait, we allow others to learn. There is an old but true saying: everything comes to those who wait.

Change in a community needs to be done sensitively and with education. When people know why something is done, they are more receptive and cooperative to whatever is being changed. Let me tell you a story about some older Catholic parishioners in a downtown church. A new pastor had been assigned to the parish. After two weeks of celebrating the daily noon Mass, he was at his wit's end. The people in the assembly did not respond to the prayers of the liturgy at all, but sat there mumbling their prayers and clanging their rosary beads against the pews. Father could no longer take it.

One day, he came out on the altar before the Mass and asked the people if he could speak candidly with them. They responded "Yes." He asked them to think about a question he was about to ask. He started: "Say you invited me to dinner and I accepted. But when I arrived at your house, you answered the door with the telephone in your hand and up to your ear, and you spoke with the person on the phone from the minute I walked in the house to the minute I left; you spoke to the person on the phone all while you served me a drink, dinner, and even dessert. Do you think I would have felt welcome in your home?"

Those assembled there all said "No!" The pastor then said, "Please listen carefully to what I am going to say next. The rosary is a wonderful devotion and has a prominent place in your life. It shows that you have a great devotion to the mother of Jesus. In our liturgy, however, Jesus is trying to speak to you both in the Word and in the Eucharist. While Jesus is trying to speak to you, you are on the 'phone' with Mary. I'd like to suggest that you come early or stay a little later to pray the rosary. While you are here to participate in the eucharistic liturgy, listen to the Word of God, respond to the greetings, and be open to what Jesus is saying to you here and now."

The people understood what the pastor was saying and they put their rosaries away. His image was clear and his message direct. When we want people to change, whatever that change may be, we need to be clear about what the change is and why we are going to do things differently.

Too often church leaders change things without any explanation and assume that people will do what the leaders ask simply out of blind obedience. This may be what actually does happen in many cases, but the correct way to go about any kind of change is to explain, explain, and explain again. There is a method of teaching which encourages teachers to tell the students something, then ask them to repeat what they have been told, and then tell them again. Here the idea is to repeat, repeat, repeat! You need only to watch one television commercial to see the role repetition plays in advertising.

When you move church furniture or the parish office, when you put in a new phone or security system, you need to let the whole congregation know about it, many times and in many ways. If you want the people to support the changes, you have to be reasonable and treat the congregation like the adults they are. You have to answer questions and give reasons, show how you will pay for the change, and the benefits of doing so. You may also have to give the history of where the change originated. Change which is understood is more easily negotiated.

Conclusion

I'm sure you have found that many of the suggestions in this book are not startling and make simple sense. They offer the parish community a sense of ownership. They highlight the Vatican II definition of the church as the people of God. They bring collaboration and collegiality alive, and honor the principle of subsidiarity.

If this book makes you aware that your common sense is good and will lead you to build the kingdom of God where you live, I will have succeeded. My prayer is that we might all be one in our search for ways to be user-friendly. In each of our parishes people should feel welcome both at the parish office and in the church. They should know and understand that they are important to the parish, and that nothing exists if its purpose is not connected to building the kingdom and fulfilling the two great commandments.

The words "user-friendly" never appear in Scripture. But I suspect that if Jesus were alive among us today, these words might be an active part of his vocabulary.

Questions for Reflection

1. Why do you want your parish to be "user-friendly?"

2. Do you see change as good or bad? Why?

3. What two things are absolutely necessary if you want people to change?

4. Why is patience necessary?

5. How long will it take for change to occur in your parish?

6. Is your parish leadership willing to change? If not, why not?

7. Now that you have read this book, how will it affect what you do in your parish?

Of Related Interest...

A World of Stories for Preachers and Teachers
and all who love stories that move and challenge
REV. WILLIAM J. BAUSCH

These newest tales (350!) from Fr. Bausch are not just a plateful of "literary twinkies" but an immense and varied menu with rich meals, wholesome lunches, snacks, and even "Playful Fare." They range in length from several pages to several on one page. *A World of Stories for Preachers and Teachers* should be in the hands of every preacher, storyteller, teacher, and reader—indeed, every person seeking to impart or gain wisdom.

ISBN: 0-89622-919-X, 544 pp, $29.95

Storytelling the Word
Homilies and How to Write Them
REV. WILLIAM J. BAUSCH

This comprehensive book helps proclaimers of the Good News develop their ability to weave story and Scripture together. This book provides speaking techniques and actual stories to help homilists reach the visually-oriented listener of today.

ISBN: 0-89622-687-5, 304 pp, $14.95

Homilies Alive
Creating Homilies that Hit Home
MSGR. FRANCIS P. FRIEDL AND ED MACAULEY

This book is a unique collaboration between Francis P. Friedl, a priest with over 40 years of preaching and teaching experience, and "Easy Ed" Macauley, Hall of Fame basketball star, sportscaster and public speaker, who is also an ordained deacon. The two define, explain, and exemplify ten fundamentals that will make homilies come alive for congregations.

ISBN: 0-89622-574-7, 144 pp, $9.95

Available at religious bookstores or from:

 **TWENTY-THIRD PUBLICATIONS**
P.O. Box 180 • Mystic, CT 06355

1-800-321-0411 • E-Mail:ttpubs@aol.com